Sand

Exploring the science of
everyday materials

Written by
**Nicola Edwards and
Jane Harris**

Photographs by
Julian Cornish-Trestrail

sundance

All rights reserved.
This edition published
in North America by
Sundance Publishing
P.O. Box 1326
234 Taylor Street
Littleton, MA 01460
800–343–8204

First published in 1999 by
A & C Black (Publishers) Limited
35 Bedford Row, London WCIR 4JH

Copyright © text Nicola Edwards and Jane Harris
Copyright © photographs Julian Cornish-Trestrail

ISBN 0-7608-5086-0

Printed in Canada

Sand is used for lots of different things.
Here are some things with sand in them.

Sand is used to make glass, too.

5

In the desert, there is sand
as far as you can see.

At the beach, waves break down rocks and pebbles into sand.

So a grain of sand is a tiny piece of rock!

I'm looking at sand through a magnifying glass.

I can see hundreds of tiny grains.

I can scoop up sand in my hand. When I open my fingers, the sand runs through them. It feels smooth and cool.

Some of the sand sticks between my fingers. It tickles and itches.

Watch me pour
dry sand from
one cup to
another.

I didn't spill any!

The sand in this egg timer pours from top to bottom in four minutes. Then my egg is cooked.

Yum!

This hourglass is bigger. But it works the same way.

I used a funnel to fill this bottle with sand. It feels heavy now.

I don't hear anything when I shake it.

I poured out some of the sand. I'm shaking the bottle again.

Now I can hear the sand!

13

I'm using dry sand to make a sand castle.

I'm making a sand castle, too.
I used wet sand.

The wet sand works!

Now we're pressing these things into the sand.

Look at all of the shapes!

What will happen if we drop a marble onto these trays?

The marble bangs on the empty tray and then rolls around.

The sand stops *my* marble from moving.

Now let's try to make some twigs stand up in the trays.

The twigs fall over in the empty tray.

The sand helps the twigs to stand up.

I'm planting seeds.
I'm going to plant
some in soil and
some in sand.

I wonder if
the seeds will grow
in the sand.

The seeds in both pots have grown.

But they grew better in the soil.

Sandpaper is paper with sand glued to it. It's rough and scratchy.

I'm rubbing sandpaper on a plastic plate. It's scratching the plate.

Now I'm rubbing sandpaper
on this piece of wood.
The sandpaper rubs
away the rough edges.

The wood feels
smoother now.

23

Sand is used for building.
A builder is adding this sand
to cement in a mixer.

The cement mixture looks wet and soft. When it dries, it will hold the bricks together.

Now it feels like rock.

Things Made of Sand

What other things do you know that are made of sand?

beach

hourglass

brick

cement

sand castle

sandpaper

Other Books to Read

Making Concrete shows how sand is made into concrete. Concrete can be used for making blocks, putting up buildings, and other things. (By Sarah O'Neil, a Sundance Alphakids book, 1999, 16 pages.)

From Sand to Glass tells how sand is needed to make the glass used in everyday things. (By Gerry Ellis, a Sundance Big Book, 1995, 32 pages.)

In *Sand*, find out all about sand—where it comes from, how it feels, and how it is different from soil. (By Sally Cartwright, Coward, McCann & Geohegan, Inc., 1975, 32 pages.)

The book *From Cement to Bridge* tells how cement is changed to concrete by adding gravel, water, and sand. The concrete is then used to build a bridge. (By Ali Mitgutsch, Carolrhoda Books, Inc., 1979, 24 pages.)

In the story *Roads and Bridges*, three friends play in and around a sandbox. They make a bridge and a castle, and a road to go between them. (By Roger Carr, a Sundance Alphakids book, 1999, 16 pages.)

Things to Do in the Kids Corner

Make up silly sentences. Start each word with the letters in the word *sand*. (*S*ally *a*nd *N*ancy *d*anced.) Draw a picture to go with each sentence.

Find a clear glass jar and lid. Fill the jar with two or three colors of sand, making layers of one color at a time. Take a stick or pencil and push it down the sides to make a design. Put the lid on to save your sand painting.

Push a few objects into a tray of wet sand. Make different patterns in the sand with the objects.

Fill one small flowerpot with sand and another with soil. Plant some seeds in each pot. Then watch to see which seeds sprout better.

Have a contest with a friend. In one minute, think of all the words you can that rhyme with *sand*.

Find the Page

You can find these ideas about sand on these pages: